YOUR KNOWLEDGE HAS VALUE

- We will publish your bachelor's and master's thesis, essays and papers

- Your own eBook and book - sold worldwide in all relevant shops

- Earn money with each sale

Upload your text at www.GRIN.com and publish for free

Bibliographic information published by the German National Library:

The German National Library lists this publication in the National Bibliography; detailed bibliographic data are available on the Internet at http://dnb.dnb.de .

Imprint:

Copyright © 2013 GRIN Verlag
Print and binding: Books on Demand GmbH, Norderstedt Germany
ISBN: 9783668722965

This book at GRIN:

https://www.grin.com/document/428215

Supreet Totagi

Human Green Brain Project. Simulating Human Brain Development

GRIN Verlag

GRIN - Your knowledge has value

Since its foundation in 1998, GRIN has specialized in publishing academic texts by students, college teachers and other academics as e-book and printed book. The website www.grin.com is an ideal platform for presenting term papers, final papers, scientific essays, dissertations and specialist books.

Visit us on the internet:

http://www.grin.com/

http://www.facebook.com/grincom

http://www.twitter.com/grin_com

CSC8499 Individual Project: Human Green Brain Project

Supreet Totagi

MSc in Advanced Computer Science,
School of Computing Science, Newcastle University.

Abstract. Simulating the growth of human brain is a computationally intensive task, requiring heavy CPU and GPU clusters. Considering growth in the area of Web-based simulation along with its advantages over traditional simulation technologies, this project proposes a Web-based model for simulating the growth of human brain. Also, emphasis is given to test the new, feature rich HTML5 technology in order to discourage browser dependencies or additional plugin requirement. Two categories of Web-based simulation- *remote simulation and visualization* and *hybrid simulation and visualization*, have been developed and tested in this project. Results showed that latter approach that uses HTML5 for data visualization is more efficient both in terms of overall execution time and server space consumption

1   Introduction

The emergence of World Wide Web (WWW) has created an environment in which many disciplines are being re-evaluated in terms of techniques and philosophies. The disciplines related to computer simulation are no exception to this phenomenon. The concept of "web-based" simulation (WBS) has been introduced and is currently the subject of interest for both simulation researchers and practitioners. Web-based simulation can be defined as the integration of Web with the field of simulation; it is an idea that represents an interest in simulation practitioners to exploit Web technology [1]. WBS is the interaction between client and the server's modeling and simulation tools, by making use of the resources and technologies offered by World Wide Web (WWW). A common characteristic of WBS applications is that they use a browser to support the graphical user interfaces in order to connect a user with the simulation. Ideally, the downloading of a simulation package from the server to the client should be independent of the browser. Nevertheless, the browser always has to play a significant role in the simulation process, either as a graphical user interface or, additionally, as a supporter for the simulation engine [2]. With the use of WBS, the processes of conceptualization, construction, execution and analysis of a simulation model becomes distributed. The pace of modeling is rapid as the levels of automated support for the modeling process increase significantly.

1.1 Motivation

Modern brain mapping techniques provide increasingly large volume of datasets of anatomical or functional connection patterns. Over the last decade, attempts to characterize these datasets have led to the emergence of new multidisciplinary subject to the study of complex systems, known as complex network analysis. This approach has its origin in the mathematical study of networks known as Graph Theory. But unlike classical graph theory, the analysis deals with real-life networks that are very large and complex [3].

The analysis of such a large volume of anatomical data usually requires distributed computer clusters. Additionally, the use of these systems for network analysis requires scalable and robust software for data management. Software is also needed to simplify data management and make the network analysis results accessible and reproducible to a wide range of target users. Considering the above factors, building a network analysis tool that is efficient, both in terms of time and CPU power is a challenging topic. A better solution would be to make use of application virtualization tools, which separates the execution of the application (intensive resource consumption) from its interaction (lightweight).

Still quite active on the research side, the concept of Web-based simulation is maturing, with efforts been made to expand Web-based simulation to include new capabilities beyond those found in traditional simulation technology. Web-based systems have many advantages compared to classical simulation systems. Many authors attempt to list them as follows [2]:

- *Ease of use.* Obtaining data from the web is a second nature to most of the users, and also, the Internet provides an interface familiar for both interacting with and controlling a simulation. With Web-based simulation environment, the user need not be involved in utilising third party software or overheads of distributed simulation.

- *Collaboration.* Communication and interaction are critical to achieve a successful simulation project. With Web-based technology, it is possible to build environment for collaborative support, such that researchers can interact from different places, working on the simulation model over web.

- *Cross-platform capability.* The Web allows running an application on any Web browser on any operating system without compiling. The application developer need not worry about the client's configuration.

- *Wide availability.* A Web-based application can be used from anywhere in the world with an Internet connection, without having to transport hardware or software.

1.2   Project Aim

The main aim of the project is to design and develop a Web-based application that simulates the human brain development. One of the concepts related to the brain development that will be adapted in this project is axonal growth in neurons. The algorithm proposed by Kaiser et al. [4], providing a simplified model of axon growth, will be the basis for simulation.

Emphasis is given to test the new, feature rich HTML5 technology, in order to discourage browser dependencies or additional plugins. Dividing the process of simulating the axonal growth precisely between server and client will be the challenging part of the project.

1.3   Structure of Dissertation

This dissertation features 7 major sections. Section 2 will aim to discuss the background concepts related to the project. Section 2.1 describes the basic concepts of Web services and applications. Section 2.2 throws some light on Human Connectome- the network of brain. Section 2.3 and Section 2.4 describes axon growth and network motif, concepts closely related to our simulation model. The design process of the Web-based simulation application will be discussed in Section 3. Section 3.1gives more detail about the simulation itself. Section 3.2 discusses the system design of the Web application model. Implementation details of the application model will be discussed in Section 4. Section 5 gives the result obtained in this project. Section 5.1 briefs the visualized output data of the simulation. Section 5.2 attempts to evaluate the performance of different application models that were tested. Section 6 presents the conclusions. Finally, Section 7 outlines possible future work on Web-based simulation.

2   Background

This section briefs the background details related to the project. Section 2.1 is dedicated for Web services and applications; it also mentions some advantages of the new HTML5 over classical Rich Internet Applications. While Section 2.2 provides broad description of the *human connectome analysis,* Section 2.3 and Section 2.4 discuss some specific areas of connectome analysis that were considered in this project.

2.1   Web Services and Applications

Web services are application interfaces that define certain standards to allow the usage of the application by another machine regardless of differences in operating systems, programming languages, or the hardware between machines. The systems that run web services implement Hypertext Transfer Protocol (HTTP) as a standard for communication between the client and server. Therefore, messages can be read on

3

either side of the connection regardless of machine differences. Typically, Application Programming Interfaces (APIs) hosted by the service provider, are used to build web services. APIs are coded in browser supported language and there are numerous APIs available, each adopting various programming languages. Web applications are meant to run on the client's browser and are designed to reduce the workload on the client, by leaving most of the work to be processed by the server [5].

A subset of web applications is Rich Internet Applications (RIA). Web applications run according to the browser specifications, on the other hand, RIA run via plug-ins such as Adobe Flash or Java applets. Many educational resources on the web are created in Adobe Flash, a propriety format to play videos and iterative content. Though Flash is widely supported, it does not run on all the platforms. Moreover integrating Flash (or even Microsoft's Silverlight) objects into a web page is not as seamless as it is with the usage of standard HTML elements [6].

The HTML5 was initially developed to simplify the creation of web content and to reduce the dependency of additional browser plug-ins. HTML5 specifications open door to a wide range of applications including multimedia distribution, business and scientific research, thus becoming the predilection language for building web applications [7]. It introduces alternatives to Flash or Silverlight. For instance, new addition of "audio" and "video" tags allows the integration of multimedia in a similar way to how "img" tag works in HTML currently. HTML media objects offer easier options for interacting with other elements on the page as part of the default document object model (DOM). Additionally the HTML5 support for Canvas is of greater interest as an alternative to Flash development.

2.2 Human Connectome

Today, we live in the age of networks. Our day-to-day social interactions such as personal relationships, financial transactions, physical transport and travel or professional collaborations, occur within networks that evolve over time. All the above-mentioned networks are examples of complex networks with highly structured connectivity pattern and capacity for self-organization that gives rise to group phenomena. The structure and function of these network phenomena can be explained with modern quantitative models and developments in graph theory and complex systems analysis [8].

In neuroscience, though the idea that the brain as a network has deep roots, the application of quantitative models and network theory to the brain is a recent development. Progress has been made in the development of innovative methods for mapping brain connectivity. A new picture of human brain driven by technology and theoretical developments is taking shape [8].

A network is basically a mathematical representation of real-world complex system, defined by set of nodes (vertices) and links between pair of nodes (edges). In large-scale brain networks, the brain regions are usually represented as nodes, and the anatomical connections between these regions are represented as links.

The human connectome is "a comprehensive structural description of the network of elements and connections forming the human brain" [8]. There are three major aspects of the connectome, central to this definition.

First, the connectome is mainly about the structure, the finite set of physical links between neural elements. A consistent anatomical description can be obtained from various empirical methods for mapping structural connections. On the other hand, functional connectivity, which can be defined as statistical dependence between remote neural elements, is significantly more variable across time. Functional connectivity reflects changes in internal state or neural responses to stimuli or task demand.

Second, it is important to note that the connectome is a description of brain connectivity. To use an analogy, the architectural description of a building summarizes major feature of the design, but not a list of dimensions and positions of all the building blocks of the building. Similarly, in the case of brain, the connectome need not necessarily represent the exact replica of connectional anatomy to the finest level of neural elements. The connectome is instead aimed to describe the architecture of brain that ranges over multiple levels of organization. So, in order to describe the connectivity across multiple levels and scales, sophisticated methods and tools shall be required.

Third, the human connectome is not just a large collection of data. It is instead a mathematical object that fits within a larger theoretical framework and thus linking neuroscience to modern studies of network science and complex systems. New theoretical, mathematical, and statistical approaches will eventually reveal the complete organization of the human connectome and its fundamental role in cognition.

Connectome analysis has various benefits in neuroimaging research. The abstraction provided by networks can reduce the complexity associated with neural networks. Network analysis, by hiding detailed features, can help to identify similarities and differences in the organization of neural networks. Also, given the identity of network nodes as representing brain regions, both comparisons between subjects and comparisons between different kinds of networks are feasible [9].

2.3   Axon Growth

The simulation depicting the human brain development has been the primary focus of connectome analysis in this project. Axon growth along with the factors that affect it has a significant role in determining the circuitry of the brain. Molecular concentrations as well as firing patterns help in determining the direction of axon growth and where that axon forms the synapse. This process of axon growth and the associated synapse formation determine which cells in the brain communicate directly and how information is processed [4].

An axon grows away from the cell having growth cone at its tip and eventually forms a synapse (junction for sending electrical impulses) with a target cell (see Figure 1).

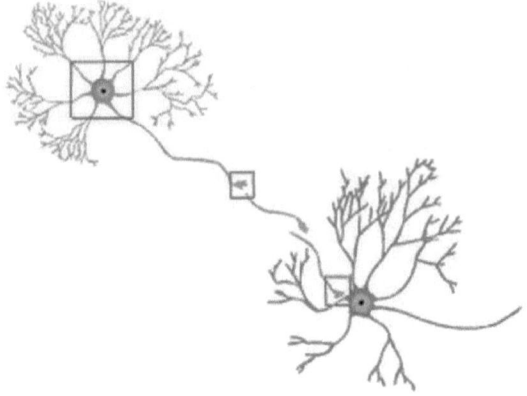

Figure 1. An axon grows away from the cell having growth cone at its tip and eventually forms a synapse [10].

A significant effort is in progress within the scientific community aimed at providing a comprehensive overview of all the factors that determine axon growth.

2.4 Network Motifs

Another concept considered as part of the simulation is "network motif". Network motifs are nothing but patterns of interconnections that occur within complex networks [11]. For example, Figure 2.4 shows the 13 different patterns how directed edges that could be distributed in a three-node subgraph.

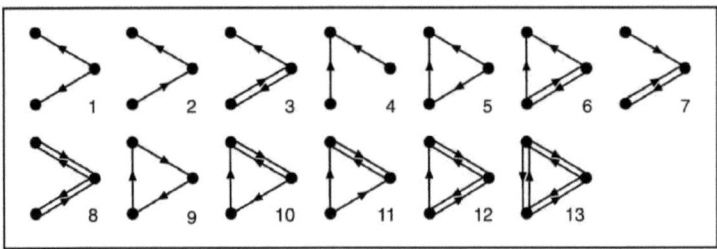

Figure 2. All the 13 possible ways to connect three nodes.

Global measures of integration rely on underlying local patterns of connectivity, which are usually diverse in directed networks. For example, anatomical triangles may consist of feed forward, feed backward and bidirectional loops, with distinct frequencies having specific implications. These local connectivity patterns are known as motifs. It is the frequency of occurrence of motif that determines its significance in the network. The frequency of occurrence of different motifs around each node is called as motif fingerprint of that node. Motif fingerprint is likely to be responsible to determine the functional role of its corresponding brain region. The frequency of occurrence of all motifs in a network represents the characteristic motif profile of that network.

3 System Design

This section outlines the overall design of our Web-based simulation system. Section 3.1 provides some in-depth details of the simulation itself. Section 3.2 describes the design of the Web application, including designs of the two models that were tested-*remote simulation and visualization* and *hybrid simulation and visualization*.

3.1 Random Axon Outgrowth

The main focus of this project was to provide a Web-based solution for simulating the axon growth. Neural connectivity appears very specific at the cellular and mesoscopic level. Though this specificity is presumed to arise from highly specific development mechanisms, there exist certain shared features of connectivity in networks by individual neurons in *Caenorhabdits elegans* or in rat visual cortex and the mesoscopic circuitry of cortical areas of human brain. In all the above-mentioned system of networks, the connection length distribution has very similar shapes. Furthermore, not each of the potentially possible synapse is formed. Only a fraction of axons, known as filling fraction, establish synapse with spatially neighboring neurons [4]. Kaiser et al. [4] explored if the aspects of these connectivity patterns can be illustrated simply by random axonal outgrowth.

Previous studies indicated that the there is a clear tendency toward low connection lengths in the wiring length distributions of various neural systems, which means most neuronal projections are short [12]. On several scales of neural systems, the probability of establishing a connection decreases exponentially with the increase in distance between neurons or regions [4].

The hypothesis by Braintenberg and Schuez (1998), called "Peter's Principle", suggests that the neural outgrowth is basically random, and the specificity in the wiring is derived from the overlap of specific neuronal population. Considering this hypothesis as a base, Kaiser at al. [4] explored whether the basic mechanisms of random axonal outgrowth can explain the connection length distributions in neural networks, with the focus mainly on local connectivity. The axonal growth cones (specialized structures at the end of outgrowing neurites) tend to grow in a straight line unless their way is obstructed by an attractive or repellant guidance cues (factors that help neurons to find the correct target cells) in the surrounding medium. A straight growing axon in a uniform distribution of neurons in a 2D space is likely to hit a neuron present in its immediate vicinity than further away. If it is assumed that the axon establishes connection with the first neuron it encounters, then the probability of establishing connection between neurons decreases exponentially with the increase in distance between neurons.

In addition to providing a model for distant-dependent connectivity of neurons, Kaiser et al. [4] also showed that the occupation of neurons introduces competition for connection targets. As a result of this competition, out of many potential connections that might occur when an axonal growth cone is closer to a dendritic tree, only a fraction of all possible synapses (actual connections) is formed.

3.1.1 Neural Connectivity Simulation

Kaiser et al. [4] tested various scenarios of synapse formation during cortical development. Out of them, the simulation of sparse neuron population was the one considered in this project. It was a condition where up to 400 neurons where randomly arranged on a 100 x 100 grid of 2D space. Only 4% of the space was filled with neurons as each cell filled 1 square unit. An axon was growing in a straight line until it encountered a neuron. Thereafter, a connection between both the neurons was formed. The axon continued to grow until it was hit by borders of the embedded space or the maximum number of synapses for that neuron had reached. An axon was considered to be close enough to form a connection with another neuron when the Manhattan distance between the axon tip and the neuron was less than 1 unit. Under what is called the occupied condition, when a neuron is already occupied with an incoming connection, other neurons were unable to establish a connection with that neuron. If the target neuron is occupied, that is, it already has an incoming connection, then the axon would grow along the same direction until it finds an unoccupied neuron (or boundary conditions).

The results of the simulation by Kaiser et al. [4] proved that assuming a straight outgrowth of axons in randomly chosen direction accounts for the exponential decay in the connection length distribution found experimentally in diverse neural networks in the primate rat brain as well as *C. elegans*. Apart from that, it was also found that spatial occupation of postsynaptic neurons and axonal competition for synaptic targets leads to filling fractions.

3.2 Web Application Model

Authors classify Web-based simulation applications into different categories: *local simulation and visualization*, where simulation and visualization take place at the client, *remote simulation and visualization*, where simulation and visualization take place at the server, and lastly, *hybrid simulation and visualization*, where simulation takes place at the server and visualization takes place at the client [2]. The model of local simulation and visualization was not implemented in our project since the current browsers, as far as our knowledge, are incapable of performing complex mathematical operations required to simulate the growth of axon. Both the remote simulation and visualization and the hybrid simulation and visualization models were implemented, and will be discussed in detail in later sections.

Though two web application models were tested, the high level design for both the models remained common.

3.2.1 High Level Design

Figure 3 shows the high level design of the web application.

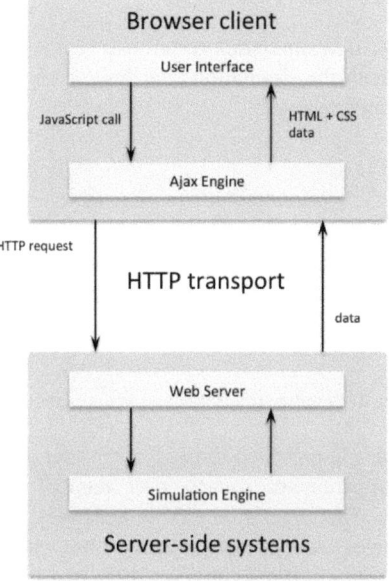

Figure 3. High level design of the Web application model.

Ajax (Asynchronous JavaScript and XML) was extensively used for asynchronous communication between the client and server. Ajax is basically a combination of several programming tools including JavaScript, dynamic HTML, Extensible Markup language (XML) and the Document Object Model (DOM), used to build interactive Web applications [13]. Unlike HTTP request, where users have to wait for the whole page to load, Ajax allows content of a Web page to load automatically when the user performs an action. The application makes use of an Ajax engine that acts as an agent between the user's browser and the server. The user's browser loads an Ajax engine instead of loading a traditional Web page, and the Ajax engine fetches the data from the server and provides it to the user. Using JavaScript to communicate, the Ajax engine continues to run in the background without interrupting the user's task on the browser.

The primary function of the web server is to cater Web page to the request of client using Hypertext Transfer Protocol (HTTP). A user agent, a web browser in our case, initiates communication with the server by making a request for a specific resource using HTTP. The request also contains the user's input parameter (number of neurons) required to run the simulation at the server. Once the Web server receives the request, it triggers the start of axon growth simulation via the dedicated *simulation*

9

engine. Once the execution of simulation engine is completed, the server responds to the client with appropriate success message (or an error message in case of failure).

3.2.2 Remote Simulation and Visualization

The first model of Web-based simulation tested was remote simulation and visualization. In this approach, both the simulation and the visualization engines, located on the server side, are executed remotely.

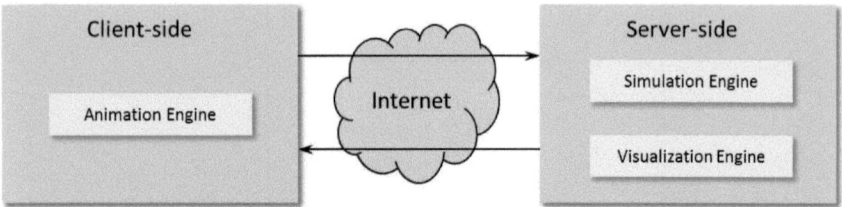

Figure 4. Remote simulation and visualization model.

Access to these engines is provided through a browser at the thin client-side. The Web server accepts input parameter from the user (number of neurons) and submits it to the simulation engine. The simulation engine generates result in the form of contiguous images. The images are sent to the client as and when generated, and the animation engine present at the client side receives these images and provides the desired output to the user in the form of animation.

The combined simulation and visualization engine was built using the algorithm developed by Kaiser at el. [4], as explained in section 3.1.1. The engine generates an image depicting the plot, neuron's position and the direction of the axon growth for each neuron. For instance, if the number of neurons provided by the user is 100, then there will be 100 images generated, each image describing the configuration of corresponding neuron. As each image is generated, it is transferred to the client-side, where the animation engine renders each image in the form of continuous slideshow.

3.2.3 Hybrid Simulation and Visualization

The second model that was tested was hybrid simulation and visualization. The approaches of remote simulation and local visualization can be combined to create a hybrid version that yields the benefit of both. Figure shows the basic hybrid simulation and visualization model.

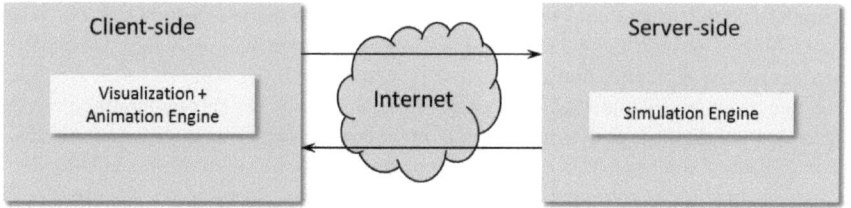

Figure 5. Hybrid simulation and visualization model.

In this method, the simulation runs remotely on the simulation server, and the visualization and animation engines are built at the client-side, which is connected to the server through a WWW browser. A dedicated data connection is established between browser and the client-side. The results of the simulation are transferred from server to the client-side, where the visualization engine is allowed to display the results to the user.

In this model, the original algorithm used to build the combined simulation and animation engines in the previous approach was modified to remove the visualization part out of it. The simulation engine received the input parameter and provided the raw data of neuron positions and the direction of the axon growth for each neuron. These raw data were passed to the client where the combined visualization and animation engine performed the rendering, in contrast to the previous approach. The visualization engine was developed using the new HTML5 technology.

There was one more additional feature added to this approach. Since the client-side provided the visualization, the browser stored the result of visualization (connectivity matrix) and the result was further used to obtain the network motifs (see section 2.4). There was another simulation engine that read this connectivity matrix and provided the raw output of network motif vector. Again, this raw data was sent to the browser and the browser rendered it in the form of bar graph.

4   Implementation

This section outlines the implementation details of the two application models that were discussed in the previous section.

4.1   Programming Languages and Tools

JavaScript, a cross-platform, object oriented language was used at the client-side. *Client-side JavaScript* extends the core JavaScript language by supplying objects to control a browser and it's Document Object Model (DOM). For example, an application can place elements on an HTML form on the fly, and respond to user events such as mouse clicks and page navigation. The main advantage of using JavaScript in our Web application is that it solves many problems such as collecting and processing data within a browser on the user's system. Nevertheless, the processed data was still sent to the server script afterward. Moreover, JavaScript is an *interpreted language,* meaning the code runs on a JavaScript interpreter within the user's browser. The code has to be just written once and it will run on any system with a JavaScript-capable browser on any computer platform.

Since productivity and efficiency of the application was key throughout the project, jQuery, a small, fast, and a feature-rich JavaScript library was used. According to official jQuery website, "it is a concise JavaScript Library that simplifies HTML document traversing, event handling, animating, and Ajax interactions for rapid web development" [14]. jQuery helped us in implementing UI related critical functionality without having to write hundreds of lines of codes from scratch. For instance, we could use a *slider* functionality that is readily implemented in jQuery as follows:

```
<html lang="en">
  <head>
    <script src="http://code.jquery.com/jquery
        1.9.1.js"></script>
    <script>
            $(function() {
                    $( "#slider" ).slider();
            });
    </script>
  </head>
<body>
```

While testing hybrid simulation and visualization model, HTML5 canvas was extensively used in rendering the simulation of axon growth, and will be discussed in detail in later section.

To define the behavior and logic of the Web application, PHP, an intuitive server-side scripting language was used. In both the simulation models that were tested in this project, the task of PHP script was to read input parameters from the client's browser, and initiate the start of simulation engine. Furthermore, the script would acknowledge the browser about the corresponding success or failure of the simulation.

The simulation engine was built using a high-level interpreted language called Octave. GNU Octave is an open source, interactive programming platform specifically suited for numerical computations [15]. Simulating the growth of axon has complex formulas and numerical computations involved, which makes Octave the most suitable tool for building the simulation engine. Additionally, Octave also provides extensive graphics features for data visualization and manipulation, which helped us to visualize the axon growth in a two-dimensional grid in our first model of remote simulation and visualization.

The Web applications were built using NetBeans IDE Version 7.3, a popular tool for PHP development, and were deployed on LAMP server, a general purpose Web server.

4.2   Remote Visualization

As discussed previously, the first method of Web-based simulation tested was remote simulation and visualization. In this section, we discuss about each module in detail. Figure shows the schematic workflow of remote visualization and simulation.

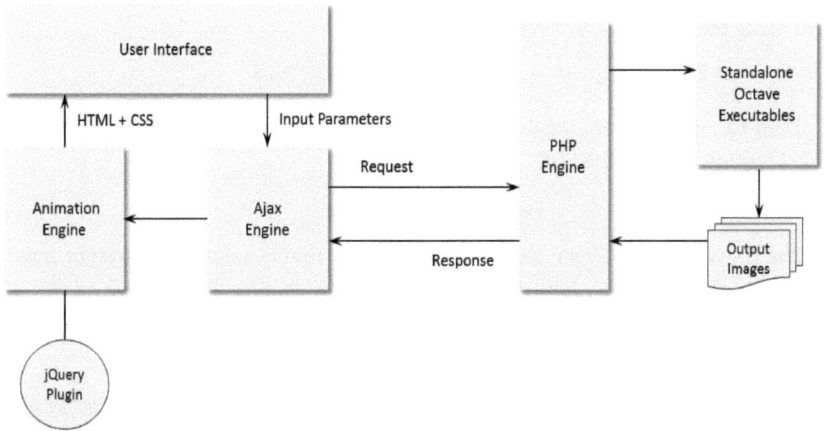

Figure 6. Low-level design of remote simulation and visualization model.

User first enters the number of neurons as input parameter through the standard HTML based Web interface. Ajax engine then comes into action and starts communicating with the Web server. The PHP engine at the server receives an HTTP request from the Ajax engine along with the input parameter. The PHP script then triggers the start of simulation engine (Octave application) using the command *exec,* a command used to run external programs.

The Octave application reads input parameter as a command line argument and starts simulating the axon growth by generating the simulation output in the form of contiguous images. Each image represents the direction of the growth of axon for each neuron.

Since it is required to generate one image per neuron, the simulation process is time consuming and due to this reason, the animation engine is started well before the simulation engine finishes executing. The client's browser receives the images from the server as and when generated, making the Web-based simulation process dynamic in nature. It is the duty of animation engine to receive the generated images, insert them into the DOM and provide animation effect for the user in order to visualize the results. Once the simulation engine finishes executing, the PHP script responds to the Ajax request with success message (or error message in case of failure), and the Ajax engine in turn sends a signal to the animation engine indicating the end of simulation.

4.2.1   Simulation Engine

13

The algorithm used to design the simulation engine was originally written by Kaiser et al. [4]. The algorithm used in this project was a slightly modified version of the original and was implemented in Octave. The first part of program is dedicated to the positioning of neurons. The program reads the number of neurons, and then a matrix of size N x 2 is created where N is the number of neurons. Each neuron, represented by each row of the matrix, is randomly assigned X and Y coordinates in the 2D grid using the following statement:

```
positions (i,:) = LIMIT * rand(1,2);
```

Then for each neuron, the direction of growth of the axon is randomly determined using built in Octave function:

```
direction = 2 * pi * rand(1);
```

The growth of axon can now be simulated by simply drawing a straight line towards the direction until it was hit by another neuron or boundary of the grid had been reached. The collision of axon tip and a neuron can be detected if the Manhattan distance between the two is less than 1 unit.

Octave provides plotting capability by access to OpenGL. It already has the default graphics toolkit library, and the plotting of neurons in our scenario was done by simply using the plot and gplot commands. The plotted graphs were then exported as *png* files as output.

Once the algorithm was designed and tested in the interactive part of Octave, it was then committed to a self-contained executable script. Executable scripts, or standalone scripts, can be used again and again on different data files. Standalone Octave scripts are written using the '#!' script mechanism. This mechanism works on GNU systems and on many UNIX systems (UNIX systems derived from Berkeley UNIX System V Release 4 and some Release 3 systems). Standalone Octave scripts are useful when a written program can be invoked without knowing that the program is written in the Octave language. In our scenario, the PHP script executes the Octave script like any other executable file simply using the *exec* command. The following example shows how an Octave standalone application can be created by using the '#!' mechanism:

```
#! octave-interpreter -qf
# a sample Octave program
printf ("Hello, world!\n");
```

The line beginning with '#!' indicates the full path and filename of the interpreter to be run, and an initial command line argument to pass to the interpreter. The operating system then runs the interpreter with the argument given and a list of full argument of the executed program if any.

4.2.2 Animation Engine

As mentioned earlier, the task of animation engine was to fetch the images as and when generated at the sever, and provide animation effect for the user to visualize the results. A third party plugin called *easySlider* [16] was used to provide numerical navigation for the generated output images. The main advantage of using a jQuery plugin is that we can integrate a common function of the plugin into any number of projects within a short period of time. Additionally, the plugin provided easy ways to set and change the transition times, transition speed and other factors affecting the animation. Apart from numerical navigation, a slider-based navigation was also provided using the jQuery-UI *slider* component.

4.3   Hybrid Visualization

The second approach towards our Web-based simulation was hybrid visualization. Figure shows the schematic workflow for this approach.

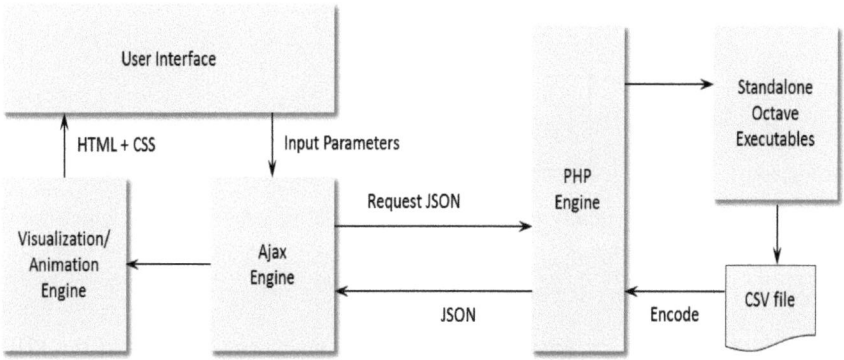

Figure 7. Low-level design of hybrid simulation and visualization model.

Similar to the previous approach the user first enters the input parameters, and the Ajax engine this time requests for the JSON (JavaScript Object Notation) data which contains the positions of all the neurons. After receiving this data, the visualization engine decodes it plots the graph on the DOM using the HTML5 canvas feature.

4.3.1   Generating CSV Output

The Octave application, as in the previous scenario, reads the number of neurons as input and generates a matrix of $N \times 2$ representing the X and Y co-ordinates of neurons. However, instead of plotting these co-ordinates in the form of figure, the matrix representing the positions is written into a comma separated value (CSV) file. Following is the sample output data taken out from the `positions` CSV file containing positions of five neurons:

Table 1. Two-dimensional array representing the X and Y coordinates of the neuron positions.

N	X	Y
1	50.00	50.00
2	53.20	3.62
3	16.39	43.30

15

| 4 | 17.19 | 41.40 |
| 5 | 93.62 | 13.87 |

Note that the first neuron is always placed at center of the 100 x 100 grid.

Additionally, the random direction of the axon growth is calculated for each neuron and is also written into another CSV file. Following is a sample output CSV file representing the direction of axon growth:

Table 2. Two-dimensional array representing the direction of the axon growth for each neuron.

N	X	Y
1	0.99	0.17
2	-0.39	-0.92
3	-0.33	0.95
4	-0.93	0.38
5	0.73	-0.68

The values in the file actually represent the growth offsets for the axon, which were calculated by the formula:

```
offset = [cos(direction) + sin(direction)];
```

Once the execution of the Octave application was completed, the task of the PHP script was to read the CSV files in the form of plaintext, encode them into JSON and forward the JSON object to the Ajax engine at the client, which in turn forwards to the visualization engine.

4.3.2 Visualization Engine

The visualization engine was developed using core JavaScript. The task of visualization engine was to read the received JSON data and provide visualization of that data to the user.

The received data contains X and Y co-ordinates starting from 0. For example, a value of 50.00 for X represents the neuron is positioned 50 units to the left of 0. Therefore, we had to first transform the received data into a form suitable for plotting onto our HTML Web page, that is, convert the data from relative format to absolute format. The next part was to render this absolute data into the DOM.

4.3.3 Rendering

Users expect webpage interactivity across the Web. For many years, the Web developers had turned to Flash-based animation for providing the interaction. But not all browsers readily support Flash, especially those browsers running on popular iPad and iPhone. Due to this reason, many Web developers now rely on the new HTML5 canvas for a wide variety of multimedia projects and visualization. It is now most widely supported standard for 2D immediate mode graphics on the Web.

HTML 5 defines the <canvas> element as "a resolution-dependent bitmap canvas which can be used for rendering graphs, game graphics, or other visual images on the fly" [17]. A canvas is basically a rectangle in our page where we can use JavaScript to draw anything on it. The markup looks like this:

```
<canvas id="graph" width="500" height="500"></canvas>
```

Every canvas has a drawing context, that is, an object that provides methods and properties for drawing on the canvas. To get the context of the canvas, we just have to call the getContext() the <canvas> element is found on the DOM.

```
var canvas = document.getElementById("graph");
var context = canvas.getContext("2d");
```

The canvas is a two-dimensional grid. The upper left corner of the canvas has the coordinate (0,0). The values increase towards the right edge of the canvas along the X-axis. And along the Y-axis, values increase towards the bottom edge of the canvas.

Plotting Neurons. After transforming the relative neuron positions from the JSON object into absolute values, the neurons are plotted into the canvas that acts like a grid of size 100 x 100. A neuron is represented in the canvas as an arc by using the arc() function. Arc in a canvas is defined by a centre point, a radius, a starting angle, an ending angle and the drawing direction. The following statement plots neurons into the grid:

```
Canvas.arc(x,y,3,0, Math.PI*2, true);
```

Axon Growth Path. To draw the path of axon growth, another canvas element was created that acted like a top layer. The bottom layer was a mere plot of neurons, and on this top layer, the actual animation depicting the growth of axon was implemented.

Each canvas has a path associated with it. The canvas provides two methods- moveTo(), to move the drawing tip to the starting point, and lineTo(), to draw a line to the specified ending point. Lastly, the continuous motion of axon growth path was achieved using the setInterval() method of JavaScript.

Additionally, the axon was said to be connected to another neuron if the coordinates of the path overlapped with that of potential target neuron. In such case, connection between two neurons is said to be formed and the connection was represented by drawing a straight line between those two neurons. The connection was stored in connectivity matrix, a two-dimensional array where each row and column represents individual neurons.

4.3.4 Building Network Motifs

Aspects of global and local brain connectivity may be characterized by individual network measure. Network measures are usually represented in multiple ways. Therefore, measures of network elements (such as nodes and links) reflect the way in which these elements are embedded in the network. A distribution comprised of measurement values of these elements provides an overall description of the network. This distribution is generally characterised by its mean. One of such measures is *motif*, the patterns of local connectivity.

In a network, the significance of a motif is determined by its frequency of occurrence, generally normalized as the *motif z-score* by comparing with ensembles of random null-hypothesis networks. There are two categories of motifs- *structural motifs*, which are small patterns of local connectivity that occur within the network with statistically surprising frequency, and *functional motifs*, which are subsets of connection patterns embedded within structural motifs [3]. In our project, we have concentrated only on structural motifs.

A freely available and open source Matlab toolbox, called Brain Connectivity Toolbox, was developed by Sporns et al. [3], which includes many recently developed network measures, was used to build network motif. The toolbox also provides weighted and directed variants for most of the network measures that are likely not yet available in other software. Additionally, the toolbox provides functions for network manipulation and included algorithms for generating null-hypothesis networks of predetermined topologies. The open source nature of the toolbox allowed us to customise individual functions according to our needs, and incorporate these functions into larger analysis protocols. We have made use of `motif3struct_bin()` function of the Brain Connectivity Toolbox to obtain frequency of structural motifs in binary directed networks.

The algorithm originally designed by Mika Rubinov (see Appendix A) to generate motif frequency vector, was modified in the project according to our needs. The algorithm initially reads the binary directed connectivity matrix that was generated during the process of axon growth simulation, and then emits the motif frequency vector, which represents the frequency of occurrence of structural motifs around a node.

The algorithm, implemented in Octave, scans the network for number of occurrences of each subgraph out of 13 possible subgraphs, and records them into a frequency vector f. The frequency vector is then written to the output CSV file. Following is the content of the sample CSV file representing the motif count for the whole graph:

```
31,108,18,24,10,8,8,6,29,10,56,17,12
```

Once this execution has completed, a PHP script then forwards this CSV output file as a JSON object to the client-side. The visualization engine at the client-side visualizes this JSON data into a bar graph using the same HTML5 canvas features as discussed in previous section.

4.4   Data Structures

During the remote visualization approach, the main output of the simulation was the generated graphical files representing the axon growth. These image files were generated as and when the virtual brain continued to develop. Database was not used since there is overhead involved in inserting and retrieving data from a multimedia database. Each of the generated image file was indexed appropriately so that the client was able to fetch these files easily and insert them into the DOM in proper order.

The main output of the second approach, that is hybrid visualization and simulation, was the positions of all the neurons and direction of growth of the axon for each neuron. This data was stored in CSV format as illustrated in section 4.3.1. When the client requests this data, a PHP script encodes the CSV into a JSON object and forwards it to the client. The following section explains JSON objects in more detail.

4.4.1   JSON (JavaScript Object Notation)

JSON is a lightweight, text-based, human readable open standard data-interchange format. Though JSON is derived from a subset of JavaScript programming language, it is entirely language independent and can be used with many other modern programming languages [18].

JSON is generally used to serialize and transfer the data over a network. Serialization is a process of transforming data structures and objects in a format suitable to be stored in a file or transmitted over a network connection. Because of this very nature of JSON, we use it to transfer data between the Web server and the Web application. The following code snippet is a valid JSON object called `positions` representing the position of neurons:

```
var positions = {values: [
          { X: ' 58.8 5', Y: '91.07' },
          { X: '51.45', Y: '16.32' },
          { X: '15.01', Y: '47.67' },
          { X: '18.78', Y: '91.63' },
          { X: '14.70', Y: '12.82' },
          { X: '95.63', Y: '16.67' },
          { X: '51.78', Y: '51.24' },
          { X: '66.78', Y: '19.96' }
    ]};
```

JSON has many advantages over traditional relational database (RDBMS). While relational databases use SQL to fetch data from database, JSON does not have any specific language to query the stored data.

4.4.2 Connectivity Matrix

In contrast to remote simulation model, where the server does all the data calculation and manipulation, the client is expected to do part of data calculation and manipulation the hybrid model of the Web application. While the simulation is in progress, the client has to continuously record the network configuration. This is done using the data structure called connectivity matrix (also known as adjacency matrix).

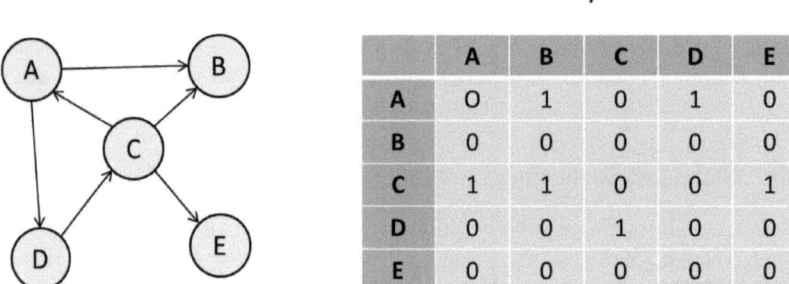

Network   Connectivity Matrix

	A	B	C	D	E
A	0	1	0	1	0
B	0	0	0	0	0
C	1	1	0	0	1
D	0	0	1	0	0
E	0	0	0	0	0

Figure 8. A five-node directed graph and its equivalent representation in the form of connectivity matrix.

The network on the above figure is represented as a connectivity matrix, which is constructed in simple steps:
- **Size of connectivity matrix:** the number of rows and columns is equivalent to the number of nodes in the network. Since the above network has five nodes, its connectivity matrix is of size 5 x 5
- **Connection:** A value of 1 in each cell represents connection between two nodes
- **Non-connection:** A value of 0 in each cell means there is no direct connection between those two nodes

This network connectivity calculated by the client is sent to the server in order to develop the network motif.

4.5 Programming Considerations

Both the models of our Web-based simulation were built and tested in Xubuntu 13.04, an operating system based on the Linux distribution Debian. Xubuntu uses XFCE desktop GUI which is stable, lightweight and configurable desktop environment. The executable version of Octave for Linux was obtained by the individual Debian distribution. Additionally, the Octave Forge packages were integrated with the development version of Octave. Octave Forge contains the source for all the functions designed to work with the Octave system.

HTML5 is the newest specification for HTML. Due to this reason, not all browsers support the HTML5 features in the same way. The table below lists the version of each major browser that supports the HTML5 along with some CSS3 features:

Table 3. Versions of each major browser that supports new HTML5 and CSS3 features [19]

	Chrome	Firefox	Opera	Safari	Internet Explorer
Canvas	3.0+	3.0+	10.0+	3.0+	9+
New Input Types	6.0+	6.0+	10.6+	5+	10+
New Form Elements	6+	6+	10.6+	5+	10+
CSS Animations	6+	6+	10.6+	5+	10+
CSS Transitions	6+	6+	10.6+	5+	9+

Like all other modern websites, JavaScript was extensively used in this project. JavaScript, a scripting programming language runs on visitor's browser and makes web pages functional for specific purposes. If JavaScript is disabled (mainly due to security reasons), the content or functionality of websites may be limited. In our case, the first step that takes place whenever the user enters input is the Ajax call. If the JavaScript is disabled in particular user's browser, then the Ajax call cannot be made and the application will simply be unavailable.

5 Results

This section summarizes the outcome of the project. Section 5.1 shows the output obtained from the Web application models. Section 5.2 attempts to evaluate the performance of the two Web application models.

5.1 Simulation Output

The output of the simulation in both the simulation models was a set of connections between neurons that were formed. The connections were represented in the form of connection matrix.

The following figure shows the visualized output of the connections formed in the first simulation model, that is, remote simulation and visualization. The number of neurons tested here was 100.

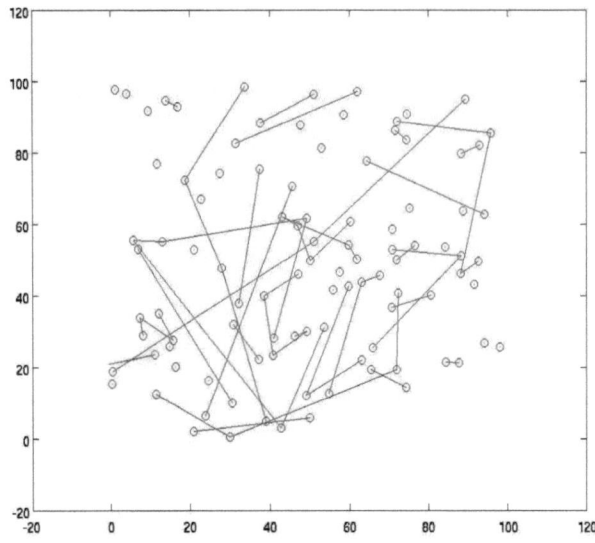

Figure 9. Simulation output of the data visualized using the remote simulation and visualization model.

As shown in the figure, an axon is represented by a straight line moving away from the spherical neuron in a constant, randomly chosen direction. A neuron forms a connection with the target neuron if the Manhattan distance between the axon tip and target neuron is less than 1 unit. Thus, the axon grows in a straight line until it is hit by a neuron or the boundary has been reached.

The graph was plotted using the Octave's Graphics Toolkit library, which has access to OpenGL. OpenGL (Open Graphics Library) is a multi-platform, cross-language application programming interface (API) used to render 2D and 3D graphics. The API interacts with graphics processing unit (GPU) to achieve hardware rendering.

The following figure shows the visualized output of the connections formed between 100 neurons in the second simulation model, that is, hybrid simulation and visualization.

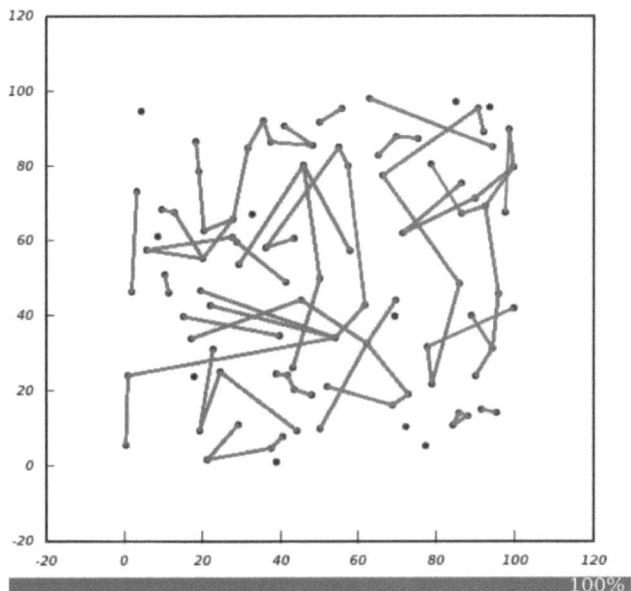

Figure 10. Simulation output of the data visualized using the hybrid simulation and visualization model.

The graph was plotted using the new HTML5 canvas element, as discussed in section 4.3.3. Since the significant part of this simulation is the connection rather than the neuron itself, the axon connectivity represented by blue coloured lines was thickened and was sharper compared to the one in previous approach. Canvas consists of a *drawable* region with height and width attributes defined in HTML code. JavaScript code accesses this area through a full set of drawing functions similar to those of OpenGL API, thus allowing dynamically generated graphics. Additionally, a progress bar was added to the functionality that represents the progress of simulation. The progress bar was implemented using the jQuery UI widget- `Progressbar`.

The connection matrix obtained at the end of simulation was used as input in generating network motif, as discussed in 4.3.4. Following figure represents the frequency vector of the network motif. The bar graph in the figure represents the frequency of number of occurrence of each of the 13 types of motif fingerprint in a three-node network.

23

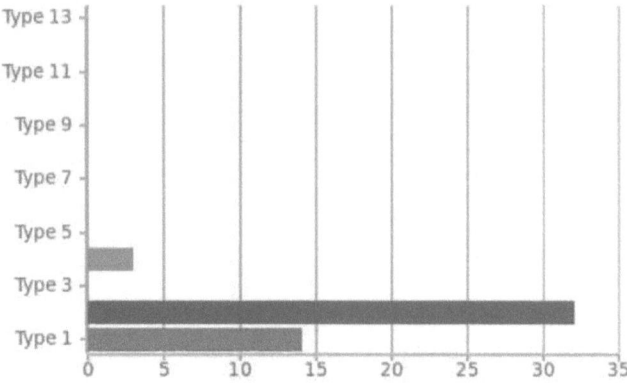

Figure 11. Bar graph representing the frequency of occurrence of 13 different patterns within a three-node subgraph.

5.2 Performance Evaluation

5.2.1 Execution Time

Figure 12 shows the time required by server to complete the simulation in the two models.

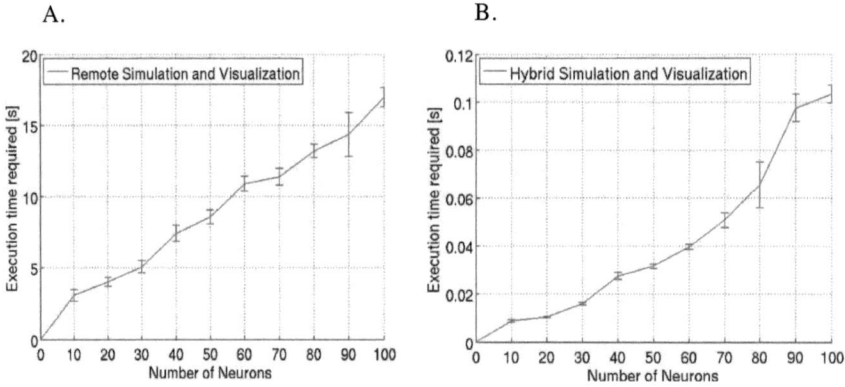

Figure 12. Execution time of simulation engines of the two models with different number of neurons as input. Vertical bars indicate the standard deviation. (A) Execution time is higher due to the influence of heavyweight graphic files generation. (B) Execution time is comparatively lower due to the influence of lightweight CSV files generation.

The execution time of the simulation was calculated for different input values for both the models. Ten trials were made for each input (vertical bars indicate the standard deviation).

It can be observed from the figure that the execution time for first simulation is much higher compared to the second one. This is because of the influence of visualization engine present at the remote server. The visualization engine generates a JPEG image for each neuron (see Section 4.2.1). For example, if the number of neurons given as input is 100, then there will be 100 images generated. Since the process of generating graphics is a heavyweight process, the model of remote simulation of visualization recorded high execution time. On the other hand, the execution time for hybrid simulation and visualization model was much less compared to the first model since the server was not required to do the visualization part. As discussed in section 4.3.1, the task of the server was just to generate the CSV file which is a lightweight process, resulting in lower execution time.

5.2.2 Space

Figure 13 shows the amount of server space (in KB) required in storing the output of simulation in both the models.

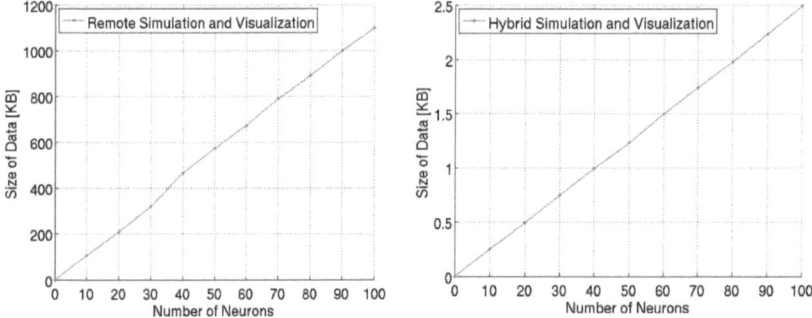

Figure 13. Server space occupied for output storage by the two models with different number of neurons as input. (A) More space is required due to the influence of heavyweight graphic files generation. (B) Comparatively less space is required due to the influence of lightweight CSV files generation.

For the case of remote simulation, the same condition of visualization influence hold true. Since the JPEG files generated as part of the output files are larger in size, the server space required to store the output is much large. It can be seen from the figure that size of output data is more than 1 MB for input of size 100. In contrast, the size of the output data in the second approach is less than 3 KB for input size of 100. This is because the output generated in this method is just few CSV files. Since the CSV files contain just floating point values in text format, their size is comparatively small and more predictable.

5.2.3 Comparison

Figure 14 shows complete run times of the Web application models.

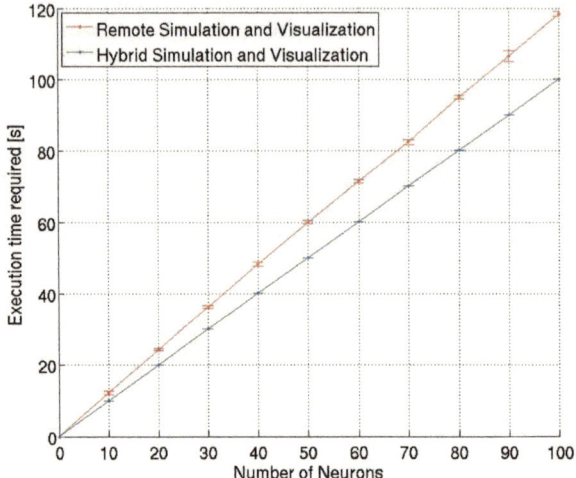

Figure 14. Comparison of overall execution time required to run the two Web application models. Vertical bars indicate standard deviation.

The transition time (time difference between axon growths of two subsequent neurons) was constant to both the applications. For simplicity, the network latency between client and server was ignored. It can be seen from the figure that the overall time required to complete one entire simulation in the remote simulation model is higher than that of hybrid simulation model for each input value. As discussed in section in 5.2.1, the increase in the execution time in the first method is mainly due to the influence of graphics generation. Since the second approach uses HTML5 canvas, the visualization happens on the fly, and there is no any additional wastage of time in generating heavy graphic files.

6 Conclusion

With the advent of technologies such as service-oriented architectures, Web 2.0 and the Semantic Web, the future holds great promises in terms of developing applications in the area of Web-based simulation. In this project, it has been discussed that utilization of Web in the area of simulation brings a number of advantages, including ease of use, collaboration, ability to control access and advantages in terms of customization and maintenance.

The report also emphasizes on discouraging browser dependencies/plugins, such as Adobe Flash, which has a limitation of cross-platform compatibility, and relying on the new HTML5 technology that has various rich features to offer.

Two categories of Web-based simulation, remote simulation and visualization, and hybrid simulation and visualization, have been developed and tested in this project. Results show that latter approach that uses HTML5 for data visualization is more efficient both in terms of overall execution time and server space consumption. This is due to the fact that the model of hybrid simulation and visualization uses HTML5 canvas for plotting the graph on the fly, unlike remote simulation and visualization that uses Octave at the server for generating heavyweight graphical image files.

There also exist some disadvantages related to WBS, including loss in speed, security vulnerability, GUI limitations, and application stability [2]. However, a number of these disadvantages are being addressed with the evolution of Web technologies. For instance, HTML5 applications which have features and functionality similar to that of desktop-based applications can be used to overcome the limitations of graphical user interface provided by the Web. Furthermore, limitations such as loss in speed can be negated by faster networks and faster servers.

7   Future Work

Several potential areas in which the project could be extended are suggested in this section.

As discussed earlier, various new features of HTML5 are designed to offer better support to Web applications. One of the disadvantages that Web applications have in comparison to the desktop applications has been the ability to store data on the local machine. HTTP cookies offer limited storage (20 cookies of 4 KB each per domain) [6]. HTML5 introduces Web storage, or also called the DOM storage. Like cookies, Web storage allows storing of data into the local machine but with larger capacity (up to 10 MB per domain). HTML5 also offers the Web applications the ability to cache frequently needed files locally. Assuming the needed data has been saved, and then the application can be run even if an Internet connection is unavailable. "Web Workers" are also part of the proposed HTML5 standard. Web workers allow JavaScript code to run in parallel rather than sequentially. With Web workers, wrong running scripts can now be written to handle computationally intensive task, without blocking the UI or other UI handling scripts [17].

The emerging technology of *Software as a Service* has also got something to offer for Web-based simulations. Using only a browser, the research data can be uploaded, shared in a controlled way with colleagues, and analyzed using the software services. e-Science Central [20] is one of the Cloud based platforms that can be collaborated with the area of Web-based simulation. e-Science Central is a Science-as-a-Service platform that combines the technologies of Software as a Service, Social Networking and Cloud Computing. e-Science Central provides a core set of services for data manipulation, analysis and visualization. Interestingly, it also allows the developers to upload their own services into the system and share them in a controlled way. Such services can be written in various languages, including Octave.

The collaboration of scientific simulations with the cloud has many advantages. The scientific work can be done entirely in private, collaborated with trusted colleagues or published openly as and when chosen. Scientists can get access to extensive scientific data and software services at a very low cost without needing to maintain their own systems or servers. With platforms such as e-Science Central, the software services can be scheduled on the cloud, making the applications more scalable and providing the ability to acquire resources only when needed. To summarize, use of cloud computing for Web-based simulations can support greater number of users, running complex scientific analysis, without having them to manage the complexity of maintaining the servers.

Acknowledgments. I wish to express my gratitude to my supervisor Dr. Marcus Kaiser for his invaluable support, assistance and guidance. I would also like to convey regards to School of Computing Science for providing excellent laboratory facilities. Last but not the least; I would like to thank my family and friends for their support during the entire course.

References

1. Ernest H. Page and Jeffrey M. Opper.: Investigating the Application of Web-Based Simulation Principles within the Architecture for a Next-Generation Computer Generated Forces Model, *Future Generation Computer Systems, 17*, pp. 159-169, Elsevier Science Publishing, 2001.
2. James Byrne, Cathal Heavey, P.J. Byrne: A review of Web-based simulation and supporting tools, Simulation Modelling Practice and Theory, Volume 18, Issue 3, March 2010, Pages 253-276, ISSN 1569-190X.
3. Mikail Rubinov, Olaf Sporns: Complex network measures of brain connectivity: Uses and interpretations, NeuroImage, Volume 52, Issue 3, September 2010, Pages 1059-1069, ISSN 1053-8119.
4. Kaiser M, Hilgetag CC, van Ooyen A.: Random outgrowth and spatial competition generate realistic connection length distributions and filling fractions. *Cerebral Cortex* 19:3001-3010, 2006
5. Thomas, T.: Design and Implementation of an Educational Rich Internet Web Application Capable of Physics Simulation within Real-Time Collaborative Interfaces. *Massachusetts Institute of Technology*, 2009
6. Godwin-Jones, R. 2010: Emerging technologies: new developments in Web browsing and authoring. [e-book] University of Hawaii, National Foreign Language Resource Center. pp. 9-15. Available through: http://www.scribd.com http://www.scribd.com/doc/52639434/Godwin-Jones-New-Developments-in-Web-Browsing [Accessed: 2nd July 2013].
7. Ganji, R.R.; Mitrea, M.; Joveski, B.; Preteux, F.: HTML5 as an application virtualization tool, *Consumer Electronics (ISCE), 2012 IEEE 16th International Symposium on* , vol., no., pp.1,4, 4-6 June 2012
8. Sporns O, Tononi G, Kötter R: The Human Connectome: A Structural Description of the Human Brain. PLoS Comput Biol 1(4): e42. doi:10.1371/journal.pcbi.0010042, 2005
9. Kaiser M. A Tutorial in Connectome Analysis: Topological and Spatial Features of Brain Networks. Neuroimage 57:892–907, 2011

10. Bean, A. n.d.. Synapse Formation, Survival, and Elimination. [e-book] http://neuroscience.uth.tmc.edu/s1/chapter09.html [Accessed: 12th June 2013].

11. R. Milo, S. Shen-Orr, S. Itzkovitz, N. Kashtan, D. Chklovskii, and U. Alon: Network Motifs: Simple Building Blocks of Complex Networks, Science 25 October 2002: 298 (5594), 824-827.

12. Kaiser M, Hilgetag CC.: Nonoptimal Component Placement, but Short Processing Paths, due to Long-Distance Projections in Neural Systems. *PLoS Computational Biology* 2:e95, 2006

13. Oracle. 2005. *Asynchronous JavaScript Technology and XML (Ajax) With the Java Platform.* [online] Available at: http://www.oracle.com/technetwork/articles/javaee/ajax-135201.html [Accessed: 25 Jun 2013].

14. jQuery. 2013. *jQuery.* [online] Available at: http://jquery.com/ [Accessed: 3 Jul 2013].

15. Gnu.org. 2011. *GNU Octave: A high-level interactive language for numerical computations.* [online] Available at: http://www.gnu.org/software/octave/doc/interpreter/index.html [Accessed: 16 May 2013].

16. Cssglobe.com. 2009. *Easy Slider 17 Numeric Navigation jQuery Slider.* [online] Available at: http://cssglobe.com/easy-slider-17-numeric-navigation-jquery-slider/ [Accessed: 15 Jun 2013].

17. W3.org. 2013. HTML 5.1 Nightly. [online] Available at: http://www.w3.org/html/wg/drafts/html/master/single-page.html [Accessed: 9 Aug 2013].

18. Json.org. 1999. *JSON.* [online] Available at: http://www.json.org/ [Accessed: 20 Jul 2013].

19. Caniuse.com. 2013. *Support tables for HTML5, CSS3.* [online] Available at: http://caniuse.com/ [Accessed: 2 Aug 2013].

20. H. Hiden, S. Woodman, P. Watson, J. Cala.: Developing cloud applications using the e-science central platform. *Royal Society of London. Philosophical Transactions A. Mathematical, Physical and Engineering Sciences* 2013,371(1983), 20120085.

Appendix

Appendix A: Program to obtain the motif frequency

```
function [f F]= motif3struct_bin(A,directory)
%MOTIF3STRUCT_BIN      Frequency of structural class-3
motifs
%
%    [f F] = motif3struct_bin(A);
%
%    Structural motifs are patterns of local connectivity.
Motif frequency
%    is the frequency of occurrence of motifs around a
node.
%
%    Input: A,   binary directed connection matrix
%
%    Output: F,  motif frequency matrix
%              f,  motif frequency vector (averaged over all
nodes)
%
```

29

```
%    Reference: Milo et al. (2002) Science 298:824-827
%
%
%    Mika Rubinov, UNSW, 2007-2010


persistent M3n ID3
if isempty(ID3)
    load motif34lib M3n ID3
end

n=length(A);
F=zeros(13,n);
f=zeros(13,1);
As=A|A.';


for u=1:n-2
    V1=[false(1,u) As(u,u+1:n)];
    for v1=find(V1)
        V2=[false(1,u) As(v1,u+1:n)];
        V2(V1)=0;
        V2=([false(1,v1) As(u,v1+1:n)])|V2;
        for v2=find(V2)

            s=uint32(sum(10.^(5:-1:0).*[A(v1,u) A(v2,u)
A(u,v1)...
                A(v2,v1) A(u,v2) A(v1,v2)]));
            ind=ID3(s==M3n);
            if nargout==2; F(ind,[u v1 v2])=F(ind,[u v1
v2])+1; end
            f(ind)=f(ind)+1;
        end
    end
end
```